This gentle book belongs to

_____
_____

Handle with care, just like Bamboo and Lita would.

I bounce out fast on tippy toes,
The morning sun is up, and it glows!
"Who's there?" I shout. "Who came to play?"
A tail goes thump-thump-thump, Hooray!

It's Bamboo Lala,
the Gentle Giant,
Big and soft, and super quiet.

She gives me one big sloppy kiss – Lickity lick! A splashy bliss!
She slurps my nose, Eww! That's how love goes!

I jump too hard. She takes a hop.
Uh-oh! Her tail just made a plop!

Her tail goes still. She turns away.
No more bounce. No more Play.

"But Mummy! I was loving her!"
Azalea gives a gentle purr.

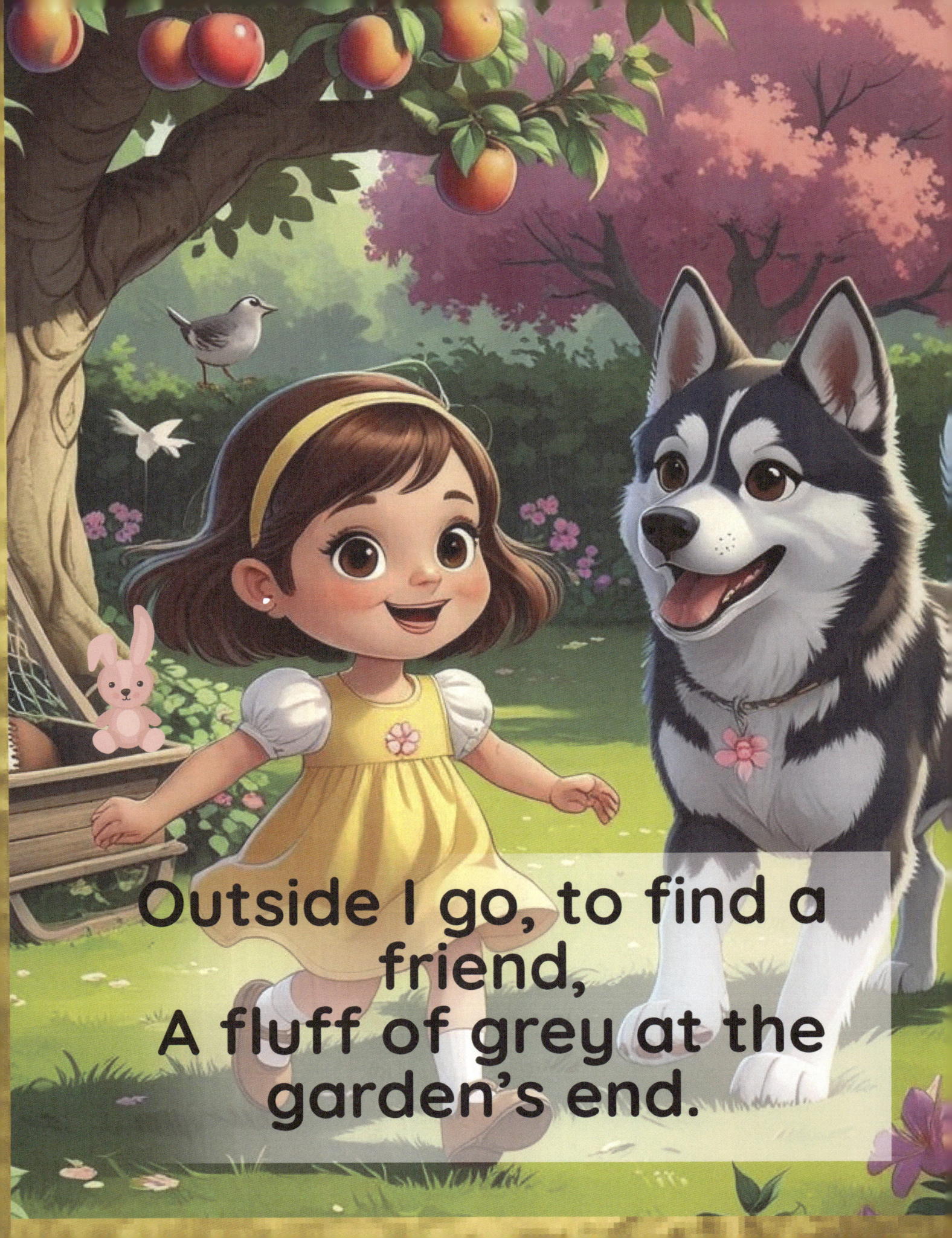

I leap ahead, SPLAT! in sand!
Now I've got dirt on every hand!
She ducks and dashes, quick and low!
I chase her fast, but where'd she go?

She grumbles low and turns her head.
She curls up near the flower bed.
"Oh no," I sigh. "I did it twice.
Why is being gentle so hard to get right?"

I sit down slow. I take my time.
No bumps, no jumps. I feel the rhyme.
Can you sit like me? Let's count to three...

Bamboo peeks with careful eyes.
Lita yawns, then softly sighs.

I stroke them both with open hands,
Soft and slow, like Mummy plans.

Goodnight, dear friends," Azalea sighs,
The stars are twinkling in the skies.

Thank you for reading my story!
I love my gentle giants sooo much, and now you're our friend too!
remember: 🎵Awooooo... no play until you're gentle, Hooray! 🎵

Printed in Dunstable, United Kingdom